First Facts

Cars, Trucks and Trains

DONNA BAILEY

M

Macmillan

How to use this book

This book tells you lots of things about cars, trains and the history of travel. There is a list of Contents on the next page. It shows you what each double page of the book is about. For example, pages 14 and 15 tell you about 'The first railways'.

On all of these pages you will find some words that are printed in **bold** type. The bold type shows you that these words are in the glossary on pages 46 and 47. The glossary explains the meaning of some words which may be new to you.

At the very end of the book there is an index. The index tells you where to find certain words in the book. For example you can use it to look up words like interchange, trestle bridges, locomotives and many other words to do with cars, trucks and trains.

First published 1988
Reprinted 1989

Material used in this book first appeared in Macmillan World Library: Travel by road and rail.
Published by Macmillan Children's Books
Houndmills, Basingstoke, Hampshire RG21 2XS
and London
Companies and representatives throughout the world

Designed by Julian Holland
Printed in Hong Kong

British Library Cataloguing
in Publication Data
Bailey, Donna
Cars, trucks and trains. —— (First Facts).
—— (Macmillan world library).
1. Railroads —— History ——
Juvenile literature 2.
Transportation, Automotive ——
History —— Juvenile literature
I. Title II. Series
385'.09   HE1021
ISBN 0–333–46640–3

Contents

Introduction

A man walked in front of this train in the 1880s to warn people it was coming! It went very slowly.

Today **monorails** run on special tracks high above the city.

a train in the 1880s

a monorail in Japan

People have always wanted to travel from place to place.

Our picture shows the history of travel. Before the wheel was invented about 5000 years ago, people walked from place to place.

About 4000 years ago they began to use ox-drawn **sledges.** Later on people used **pack animals** to carry their goods.

Rich people rode in comfort in **carriages** pulled by horses. In 1804 the first railway engine was invented.

In 1863 a French engineer built the first motor car.

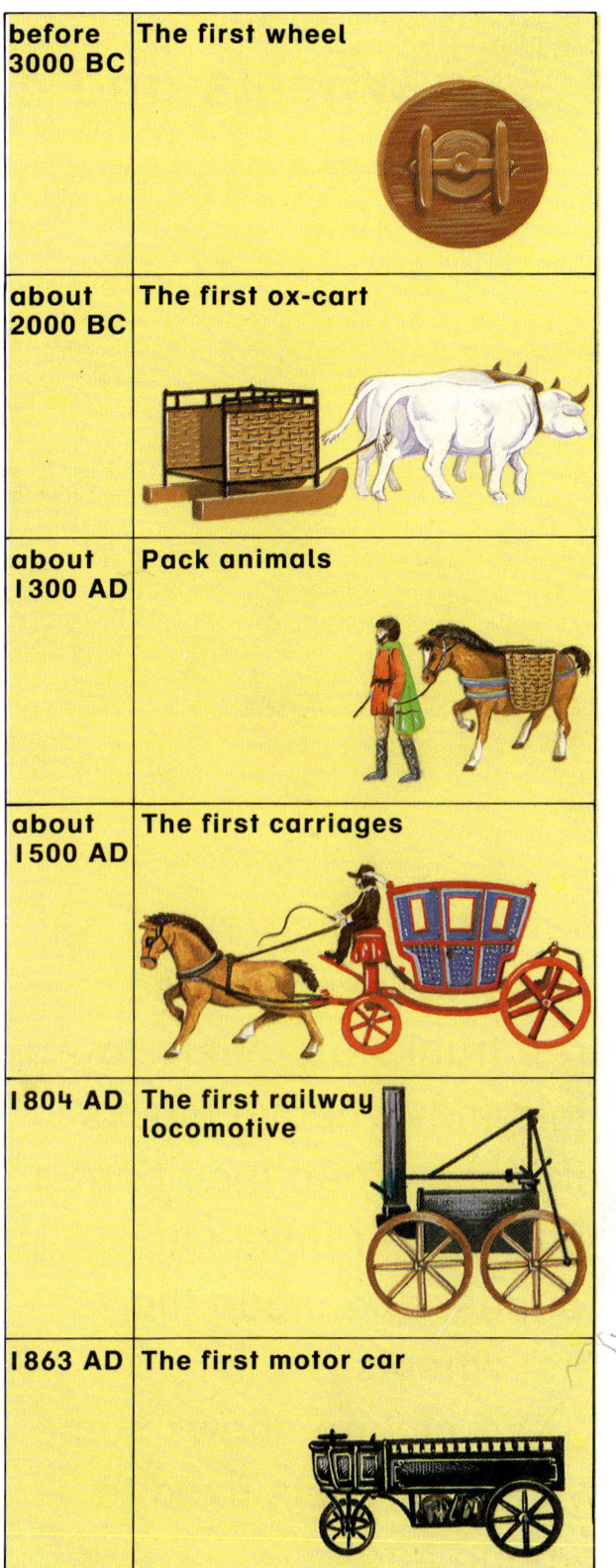

before 3000 BC	The first wheel
about 2000 BC	The first ox-cart
about 1300 AD	Pack animals
about 1500 AD	The first carriages
1804 AD	The first railway locomotive
1863 AD	The first motor car

Wheels and chariots

moving a heavy stone

Before wheels were invented, people used tree trunks as rollers to help move heavy blocks of stone. Then they began to cut tree trunks into rounds, and made the first wheels.

Our picture shows some wooden wheels fixed to a hand cart.

6

People used oxen to pull
heavy carts. Horses
pulled their **chariots** into
battle or for hunting. The
lighter chariots could go
much faster than ox-carts.
Romans raced their
chariots around a track.

an ox-cart

a chariot race

Roman roads

About 2000 years ago, the Romans
ruled most of Europe. They needed
to get to different parts of Europe
very quickly, so they built the first roads.

Our picture shows how they made
their roads by laying big blocks of
stone on a base of earth and pebbles.
Roman chariots could then go very
fast along the smooth flat surface.

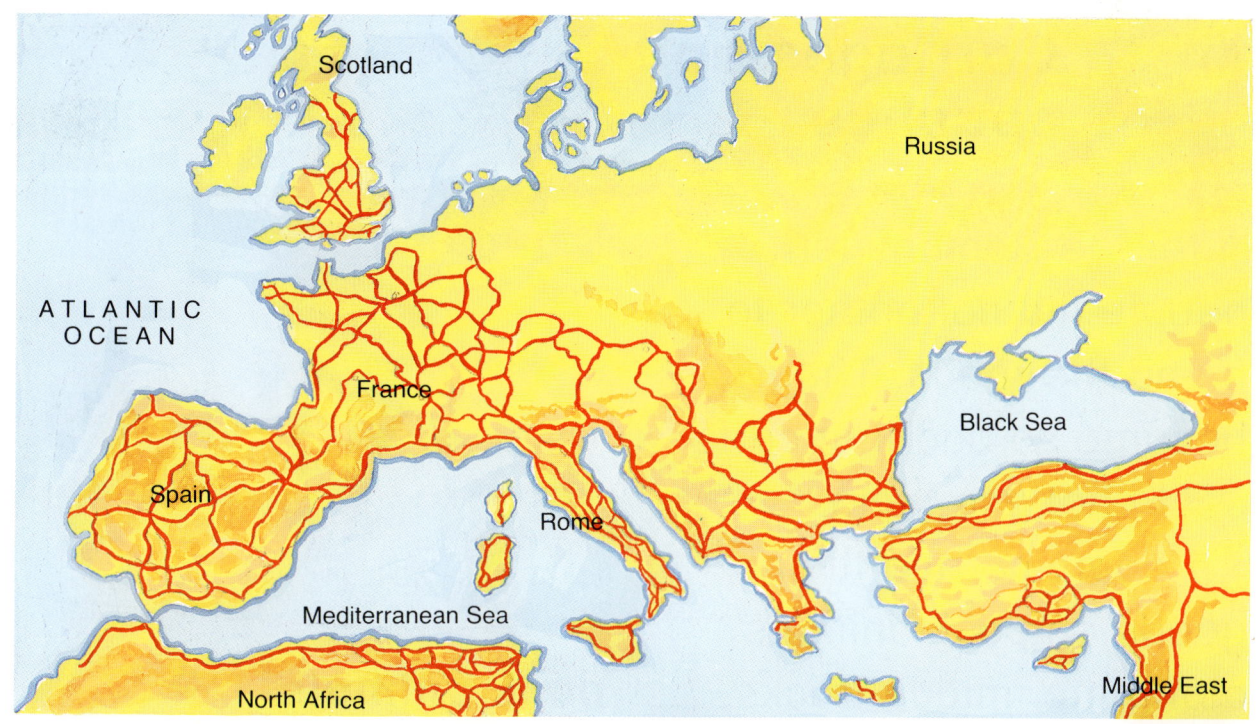

Our map shows many of the roads that the Romans built. Roman roads were very straight. Many modern roads follow the same route as the old Roman roads.

The Roman road in our picture looks the same as when the Romans built it.

a Roman road in Italy

Carriages and coaches

After the Romans left, people did not bother to mend the roads. They became so bad that carts could not use them.

People carried their goods on pack animals along the muddy tracks.

pack animals

a rich man's carriage

Later people began to improve the roads and rich people travelled along them in their splendid carriages. People with less money travelled together in stage coaches.

Stage coaches travelled long distances between towns. They carried passengers and mail, and stopped at inns to change the horses.

Our picture on this page shows two stage coaches outside an inn.

The American West

When people began to explore America they travelled together in **wagon trains.**

The red lines on our map show the **wagon trails** to the West.

a circle of wagons

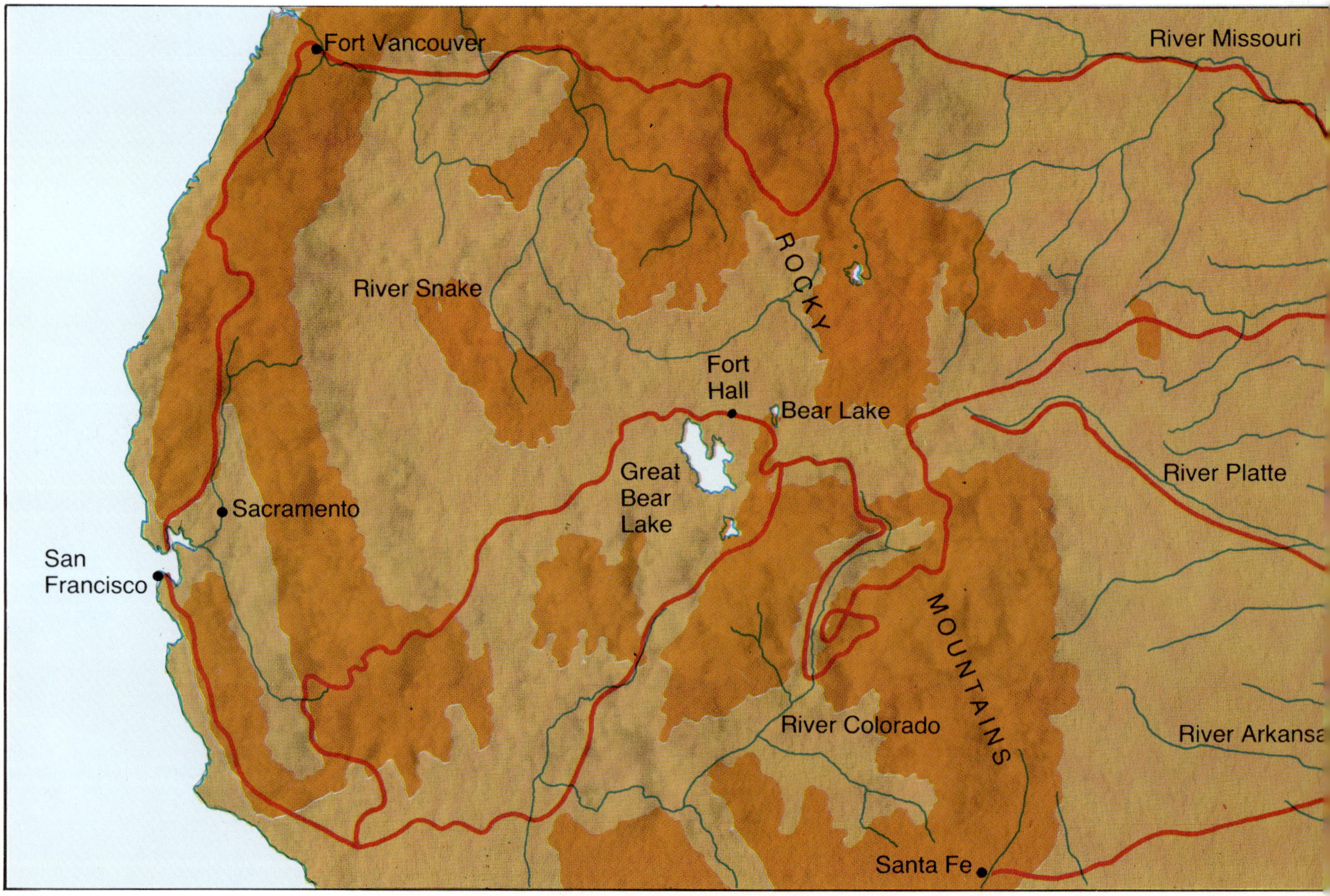

Fort Vancouver

River Missouri

River Snake

ROCKY

Fort Hall

Bear Lake

Great Bear Lake

River Platte

Sacramento

San Francisco

MOUNTAINS

River Colorado

River Arkansas

Santa Fe

crossing a river

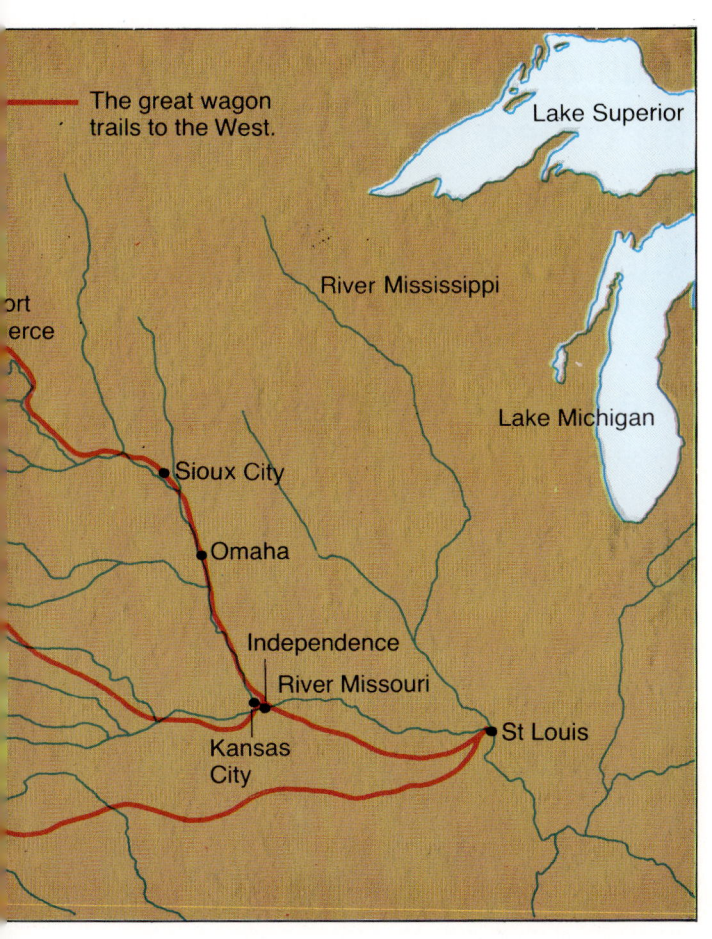

The great wagon trails to the West.

Lake Superior

River Mississippi

Lake Michigan

ort
erce

Sioux City

Omaha

Independence

River Missouri

Kansas
City

St Louis

The travellers lived in their wagons. At night they made a circle of the wagons and lit a fire in the centre to frighten away wild animals.

It was a hard life, and they were often cold and hungry.

Crossing a river was often dangerous. The wagons got stuck in the mud, or rocks broke their wheels. Then the whole wagon train would stop until the broken wheel was mended.

People used to cross America like this in wagon trains until the first railways were built.

The first railways

Richard Trevithick invented the first railway engine in 1804, but it could not travel very far.

George Stephenson built an engine called the 'Locomotion' in 1825.

Our picture shows it pulling the first passenger train. The passengers sat in open carriages.

Stephenson's 'Rocket'

In 1829 Stephenson built a faster engine which he called the 'Rocket'. It could travel at 46 kilometres per hour.

the first passenger train

An engine called 'The Best Friend of
Carolina' was built in America in 1830.
It had a tall chimney so the smoke
could go high up into the air. The
passengers sat in closed carriages
to protect them from the smoke and
sparks from the chimney.

Railways worldwide

In England, Brunel built railway lines, tunnels and bridges. In America, more powerful engines, like the 'Lafayette', built in 1837, ran on the new railways.

this tunnel was built in 1835

the 'Lafayette'

LAFAYETTE

B.&O.R.R.

Soon railways were being built all over Europe, Canada and America. The first railways in America were only on the East coast.

In 1864 work began on a railway to cross America from East to West. It took five years to build. People could then travel much faster across the Rocky Mountains.

Sometimes the engine broke down and the passengers had to wait until the driver and engineer could mend it.

Building bridges

Railway lines often had to cross
rivers and deep valleys, so engineers
built bridges across them.

Some bridges are very large, like
the **trestle** bridge in our picture.
Trestle bridges were first made of
wood, but now they are made of steel.

Railway bridges must be very strong to carry the weight of the heavy trains which cross over them.

Our picture shows one of the largest railway bridges in the world, which was built in 1890 across the Firth of Forth in Scotland.

It has three huge **spans** made of strong steel **girders.**

The first cars

Our picture shows a steam wagon, built in 1796 to carry heavy loads. It had three heavy wooden wheels and did 3 kilometres per hour (kph).

In 1885, a German, Karl Benz, built the first car to have a petrol engine. It had three bicycle wheels and could travel at 13 kph.

By 1899 cars were faster and more comfortable, like the Fiat in our picture, which had four wheels, rubber tyres, and could carry four people, but they got very wet in the rain!

the Benz,
1885

the Fiat,
1899

Motoring for the rich

The first cars were sold to rich people who had their cars made specially for them. The cars had no windscreens, so the **chauffeur** sat on his own in front. The passengers sat in the back on comfortable leather seats and were more protected from the weather.

The Mercedes in our picture was made in Germany in 1904.

a 1907
Napier

a 1903
Cadillac

People driving open cars like this
Napier wore special clothes and
goggles to keep out the dust. In
America this 1903 Cadillac was one
of the most popular cars.

Henry Ford

Early cars were made one at a time.
Then Henry Ford started a factory in
Detroit to make cars, and in 1908 he
made a new car called a Model T.

Ford worked out a way of making
Model Ts cheaply, on a **production line.**

Every worker only did one job on the
car, so the car was finished faster
and cost less to make.

Ford sold over 15 million Model Ts.

Ford cars have changed since 1908.
The Ford Thunderbird in our picture
was a popular sports car in 1955.
People still buy Ford cars today.

**a 1955
Thunderbird**

'The Century'

Business people want to travel quickly between big cities. In the 1930s in America they travelled in a train called 'The Century'. It ran every day between New York and Chicago.

The red line on our map shows the **route** of the railway.

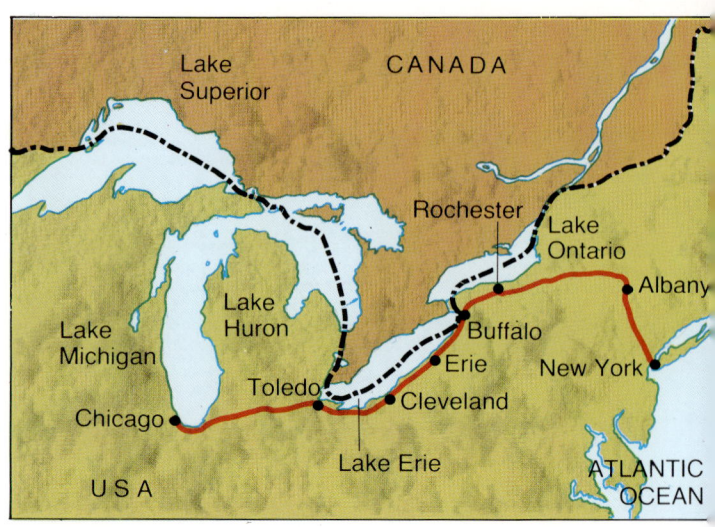

At first 'The Century' was pulled by a huge steam **locomotive,** the 4-6-4 Hudson which was **streamlined** to make it go faster.

'The Century'

the Hudson steam locomotive

After 1948, three **diesel** locomotives pulled 'The Century'. The journey between New York and Chicago took 16 hours.

Today you can go by plane in 3 hours. No one needs 'The Century' any more so it no longer runs.

Railways of the world

There are many other famous trains in the different countries of the world. People can cross continents in them.

The Canadian Pacific train crosses the Rocky Mountains. It has special viewing coaches for the passengers to see the scenery.

The Indian Pacific runs from East to West across Australia.

Our chart shows the names of some of the world's most famous trains.

Some Famous Trains				
Train	Country/Continent	Route	Distance (km)	Average Speed (kph)
Canadian	Canada	Montreal to Vancouver	4800	70
Flying Scotsman	United Kingdom	London to Edinburgh	640	128
Indian Pacific	Australia	Perth to Sydney	3970	62
Mistral	France	Paris to Nice	1090	120
Orient Express	Europe	Paris to Istanbul	3000	44
Russia	USSR	Moscow to Vladivostok	9438	48
Shinkhansen Hikari	Japan	Tokyo to Osaka	517	162
Twentieth Century Limited	USA	New York to Chicago	1540	96

the
Canadian
Pacific

the Indian
Pacific

Motorways

Just as cars have changed, so have the roads that people drive on. Today every country has a network of **motorways** and their **interchanges,** where the motorways join each other.

Our picture shows a motorway interchange at San Diego in America.

In Germany, many of the interchanges have a 'cloverleaf' pattern.

a motorway interchange

Our picture above shows the entrance to a French motorway, where you pass through a barrier and collect a ticket. When you leave the motorway, you pay for the distance you have travelled.

a cloverleaf junction

Cars today

Most European cars are smaller than American cars and use less petrol.

The Mini Metro is a popular car in Britain because it is cheap to run and easy to park.

The Citroen BX is a popular family car in France because it is easy to repair the bodywork.

a Mini
Metro

a Citroen
BX

a Porsche 911

Sports cars, like this German Porsche 911, and luxury cars like the Cadillac are both expensive to buy and they also use a lot of petrol.

a 1985 Cadillac

Trucks and freight

With better roads, people built larger and larger trucks to carry the **freight** across continents.

Our picture shows a large American truck with a trailer behind it. The truck has a cabin behind the driving compartment where the driver can sleep on long journeys.

Factories pack their goods into **containers** which are lifted onto the back of lorries.

Our picture shows a **hoist** unloading a lorry at the docks.

Road trains with three or more **trailers** carry freight across the Australian desert.

a container on a lorry

road trains in Australia

Car racing

Racing cars have small bodies and large wheels to grip the track. The wheels often need changing during a race, because the rubber on the tyres wears thin.

The driver pulls into a **pit stop** at the side of the track and the **mechanics** change the wheels in less than ten seconds.

racing in the 1930s

In the 1930s, cars raced at Brooklands on a track which was **banked** up to allow the cars to go round the corners faster.

At the start of the 1985 Portugal **Grand Prix** race, the cars jostled to get into a good position.

racing in 1985

High speed trains

Modern high speed trains run on special tracks, which are long and straight with only gentle curves.

The Canadian high speed train in our picture is called a Turbo or **LRC.** It has a top speed of about 200 kph.

The French high speed train, the **TGV,** runs on special tracks. It can reach a speed of 300 kph.

Japanese high speed trains are called Bullet trains, because of their shape and speed. Bullet trains have a top speed of 250 kph.

the French TGV

a Bullet train

The record breakers

Vehicle		Speed
1825 The Rocket United Kingdom		
1848 The Great Britain United Kingdom		
1893 Empire State Express No 999 USA		
1938 Mallard United Kingdom		
1981 TGV France		
1979 Maglev test train Japan		

kph   100   200   300   400

mph   100   200

1885 Benz Tricycle Germany		Karl Benz
1899 Jamais Contente France		Jenatzy
1904 Gobron-Brillie France		Louis Rigolly
1927 Sunbeam United Kingdom		Henry Segrave
1947 Napier-Railton United Kingdom		
1964 Spirit of America USA		
1970 The Blue Flame USA		
1983 Thrust 2 United Kingdom		

40

Over the years, makers of trains
and cars have competed to build the
fastest trains and cars.

At first trains went faster than
cars, but our table shows that now
there are cars which are built to
win the world land speed record.
These cars have rocket engines
instead of ordinary petrol engines.

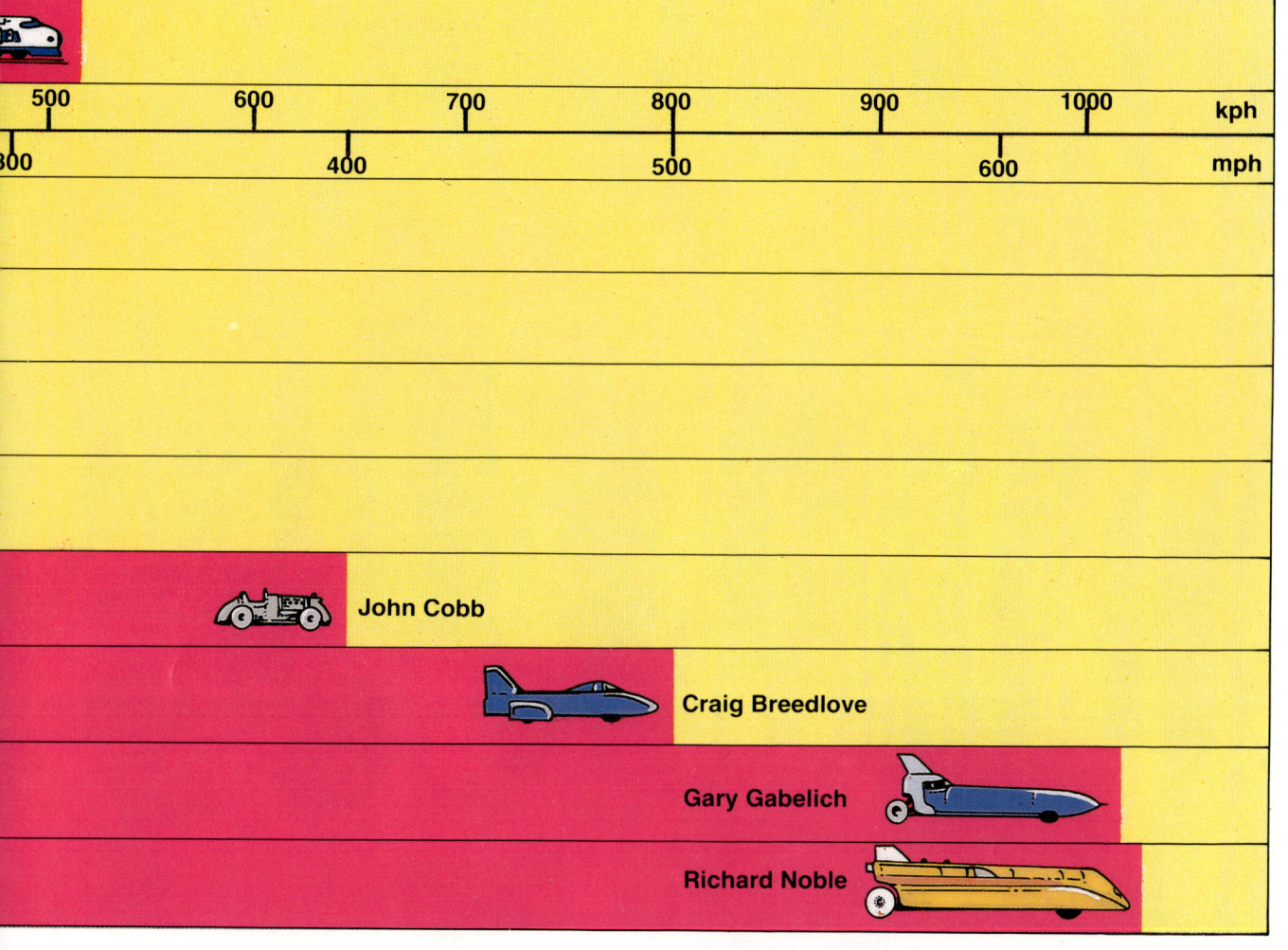

| | 500 | 600 | 700 | 800 | 900 | 1000 | kph |
| 300 | | 400 | | 500 | | 600 | mph |

John Cobb

Craig Breedlove

Gary Gabelich

Richard Noble

Safety on road and rail

Now that trains travel so fast, it is important to make sure there are no accidents. Trains must not crash into each other.

These traffic controllers in France use computers and a large plan of the railway tracks. The lights on the plan show the speed and position of every train.

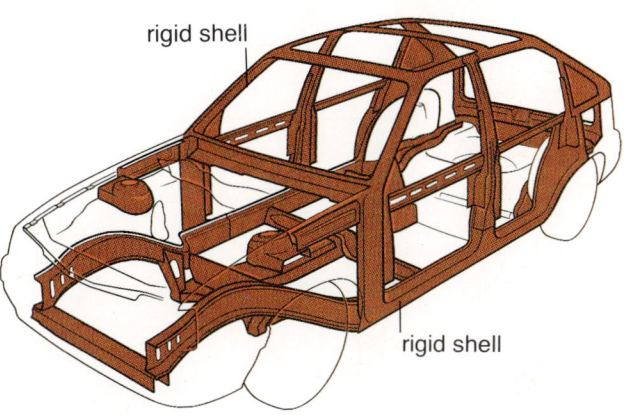

testing a car

Car manufacturers build cars with steel frames so that they do not crumple up in an accident. This helps to prevent injury to the passengers. They test the cars with dummy people to see what happens.

a car's steel frame

rigid shell

rigid shell

Looking ahead

Electric cars are clean and quiet.
Our picture shows an electric car in
Amsterdam, which the Dutch are
using to help solve the problems of dirt,
noise and traffic jams in the city. But
we need to develop electric cars that
can go long distances before people
will really want to buy them.

**an
electric car**

A new train, the Maglev, is now being developed in Japan. It runs on a special kind of track. The train is raised off the track by **magnets,** so there is a cushion of air underneath it. More magnets pull the train forward.

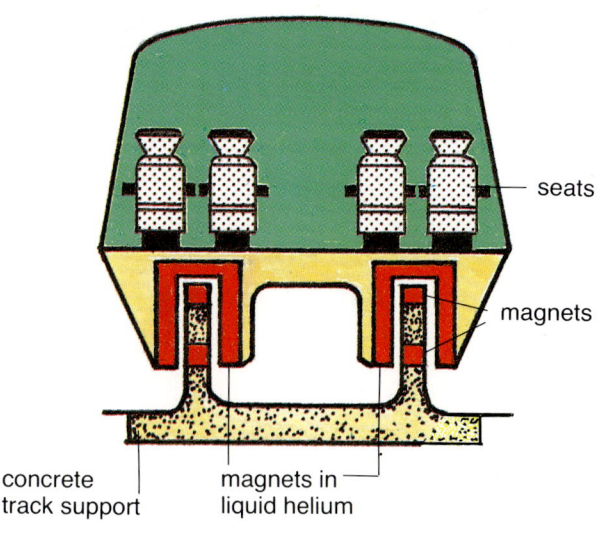

seats

magnets

concrete track support

magnets in liquid helium

the track of the Maglev

a model of the Maglev

Glossary

banked built up so that it slopes upwards on bends.

carriage a wheeled vehicle for carrying people, usually drawn by horses, also a railway passenger vehicle.

chariot a light, two-wheeled cart pulled by one or more horses. Chariots were used for war, for hunting and the Romans used them for racing.

chauffeur a person whose job is to drive a car for someone.

containers large metal boxes which are packed with goods at a factory so that the goods can be more easily moved from place to place.

diesel a type of engine that burns heavy oil. The diesel engine was invented by Rudolf Diesel.

freight the goods carried by any form of transport.

girders the metal supports of a bridge.

goggles glasses which protect the eyes.

Grand Prix French for 'big prize'. Grand Prix races are held in 10 countries of the world. Racing car drivers win points in each race. The driver with the most points at the end of the year becomes the world champion.

hoist a mechanical lift.

interchange where traffic can join or leave a motorway from another road, or where two motorways meet and join.

locomotive an engine which pulls a train.

LRC standing for 'Light, Rapid and Comfortable' this is the Canadian high speed train with a top speed of about 200 kph.

magnet a piece of iron or steel made to attract or repel another piece of iron.

mechanics people who work with machines.

monorail a train which runs on a single track. The train sits astride the track and electric motors turn the driving wheels.

motorways the British name for roads which are specially built to carry fast motor traffic in safety. Motorways have gentle slopes and curves, with at least two or three lanes of traffic going in each direction. The traffic lanes are usually separated by a barrier.

pack animals animals such as horses, donkeys and mules, which carry goods on their backs.

pit stop a place beside the main race track where a driver can pull out of the race to have the wheels replaced and the car checked by mechanics.

production line a moving belt in a factory, where each worker does only one special job on the production of each car.

road trains large trucks in Australia which each have two or three large trailers. Road trains usually travel together across the desert.

Romans the Romans lived in Italy about 2000 years ago. They ruled most of Europe and North Africa for about 400 years. They were good soldiers and engineers and built many roads.

route the way from one place to another.

sledges carts with wood or metal runners instead of wheels.

spans the arches of a bridge.

streamlined something designed to allow the air to flow smoothly around it, so that it can move forward faster.

TGV Train de Grand Vitesse, French for high speed train.

trailers large wheeled units with no engines, pulled by trucks.

trestle a wooden or metal criss-cross framework that supports a road or railway bridge.

wagon trails tracks used by the wagon trains across wild country.

wagon trains groups of wagons travelling together.

Index

Acknowledgements
The Publishers wish to thank the following organizations for their invaluable assistance in the preparation of this book: Adam Opel AG; Austin Rover; Australian Information Service, London; Canadian Pacific; General Motors (Adam Opel AG); General Motors (Cadillac); General Motors (Vauxhall-Opel); Japan National Tourist Organization; Porsche Cars; Renault UK; SNCF – French Railways.
Photographic credits (*t*=top *b*=bottom *l*=left *r*=right)
Cover photograph J. Allan Cash and Colorific; title page J. Allan Cash; 4*t* Mansell Collection; 4*b*, 9*b* ZEFA; 11 The Bridgeman Art Library; 14*t*
ZEFA; 14/15, 16*t* The Bridgeman Art Library; 17 Mansell Collection; 19 ZEFA; 21*t* 21*b*, 22, 23*t*, 23*b*, 24, 25 The National Motor Museum, Beaulieu; 27 Victor Hand; 29*t* Canadian Pacific; 29*b* Australian Information Service, London; 30 ZEFA; 31*t* Loek Polders; 31*b* ZEFA; 32*t* Austin Rover; 32*b* Loek Polders; 33*t* Porsche Cars; 33*b* General Motors (Cadillac); 34, 35*t*, 35*b* ZEFA; 36, 37*t*, 37*b* L.A.T. Photographic; 38 ZEFA; 39*t* SNCF French Railways; 39*b* Japan National Tourist Organization; 42 SNCF – French Railways; 43*t*, 43*b* General Motors (Adam Opel AG); 44 Loek Polders; 45*b* Japan National Tourist Organization.